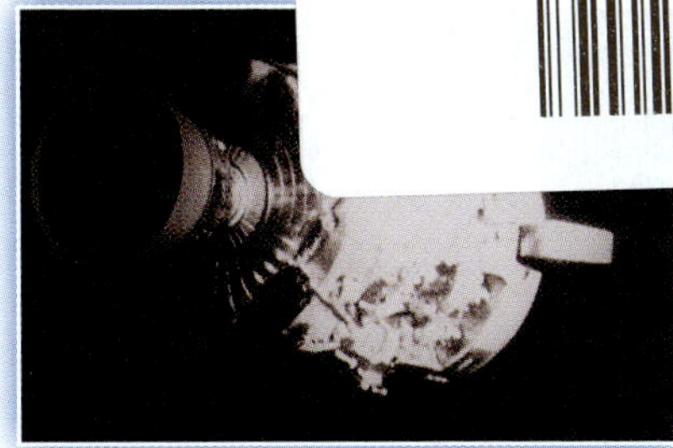

TROUBLE IN SPACE

by Gloria Jasperse

HOUGHTON MIFFLIN HARCOURT
School Publishers

PHOTOGRAPHY CREDITS: **Cover** © NASA David Scott. **1** NASA Marshall Space Flight Center. **2** © Tiziou Jacques/CORBIS SYGMA. **3**3 (l) NASA, (r) NASA. **4** NASA Marshall Space Flight Center. **5** NASA - Apollo/digital version by Science Faction. **6** © NASA/Roger Ressmeyer/CORBIS. **7** Science Faction/Getty Images. **8** NASA Marshall Space Flight Center. **9** © CORBIS. **10** © Bettmann/CORBIS. **11** NASA David Scott. **12-13** NASA. **14** NASA

Printed in India

ISBN-13: 978-0-547-02414-1
ISBN-10: 0-547-02414-2

2 3 4 5 6 7 8 0940 18 17 16 15 14 13 12 11 10

For many years, people knew very little about the moon and outer space. Some people studied astronomy to learn about the moon and the stars. They learned about the orbit of the moon and the planets. Then, in 1969, astronauts explored the moon for the first time.

In 1970, a group of astronauts prepared to explore the moon again.

Their mission was called Apollo 13, and the astronauts were well prepared. James Lovell was the mission commander. He was in charge of the entire mission. Fred Haise was the lunar module pilot. John Swigert was the command module pilot.

All three astronauts planned to fly to the moon in the command module. Then, the command module would orbit while two astronauts flew down to the moon to the lunar module.

Command module

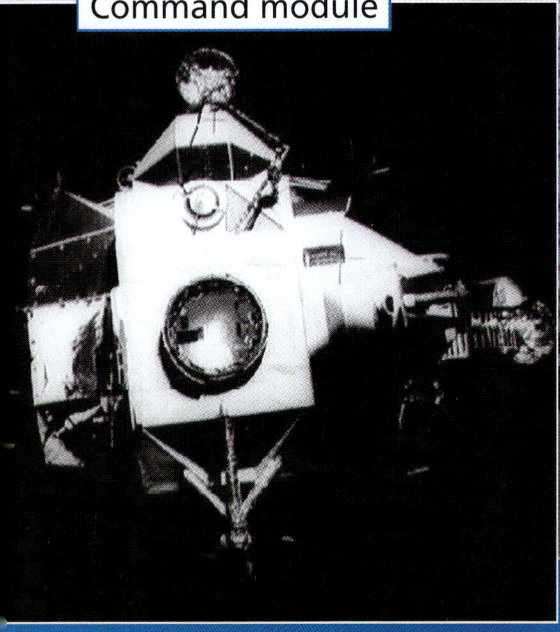

Lunar module

Apollo 13 launched into space on April 11, 1970. As the rocket sped away from Earth, everything went well. Each of the astronauts had a job to do. After they entered space, they talked to mission control to report on their progress. They worked on experiments and reported to the crew back on Earth.

The crew of Apollo 13 wanted to share their trip with people on Earth. So they filmed a TV program inside Apollo 13. They talked about living inside the space capsule and being weightless in space. At the end, Commander Lovell wished everyone a good night. Then they sent their program back to Earth. They hoped it would be shown on TV.

But the TV stations decided not to show the TV program that the astronauts had made. They thought people would be bored by the Apollo 13 mission. Many people had already seen pictures of objects floating without gravity. They didn't think the Apollo 13 mission would be anything new or exciting.

But traveling in space was still exciting, and it was also very dangerous.

Floating in space

Nine minutes after they finished making their TV program, the crew of Apollo 13 heard a loud noise. They didn't know what the noise was, but no one was worried. Fred Haise often played jokes by making loud noises, and the other astronauts thought it was another one of his jokes.

But it was not a joke. It was the explosion of an oxygen tank. This caused other things to break. The spacecraft could no longer produce electricity or water or supply more oxygen. The crew needed oxygen to breathe, water to drink and to operate the craft, and electricity to travel back to Earth. The Apollo 13 crew was in serious trouble. They would have to stop their mission and find a way to return to Earth right away.

The astronauts knew there was a backup battery. The backup battery could provide energy for 10 hours. But they would need to use that energy to enter Earth's atmosphere, and they were 87 hours away from Earth! They needed to find a way to generate energy, oxygen, water, and return to Earth.

"Houston, we've had a problem," Commander Lovell said. These were words that Mission Control did not want to hear. It meant that the crew of Apollo 13 was in trouble. Their distance from Earth would make it even more difficult to fix the problem.

The Apollo 13 crew would have to work quickly to repair the damage. They could not stay in the command module because energy was running low. They moved out of the capsule and into the lunar module because this would save energy. They would need all of their energy to return to Earth.

However, the lunar module was built to hold two people. Now all three astronauts would need to live in this small space.

The lunar module also had no heat, so it was very cold. The water supply was almost gone, and there was not much oxygen. The astronauts began to worry about the future of Apollo 13. They worked with Mission Control to fix the problems and get back to Earth.

The astronauts forced the module in the right direction. They did not drink a lot of water, and they used tape to stop things from floating around. They still had a long way to go, but it looked like they were on their way home.

Now the TV stations were showing programs about Apollo 13. The entire county wanted to know what was going to happen to the astronauts on that mission.

On April 17 at 1:07 P.M., the crew of Apollo 13 splashed down in the Pacific Ocean. They were safe. The astronauts and Mission Control had worked hard to get Apollo 13 back home. Everyone cheered when they landed!

Responding

TARGET SKILL Text and Graphic Features What do the photos in this book show you about Apollo 13? Copy the chart. First list a photo from the book. Then list the page where the photo appears. Then list what the photo shows you about Apollo 13.

Photo	Page	Purpose
Rocket lift-off ?	Page 4 ?	Travelled to outer space ?

Write About It

Text to Self Use a few sentences to write a response paragraph telling why you would or would not like to travel in space. Include details about how it might feel, look, and sound in space.

TARGET VOCABULARY

astronomy	future
explored	orbit
float	repair
force	space

TARGET SKILL **Text and Graphic Features** Tell how words go with photos.

TARGET STRATEGY **Analyze/Evaluate** Tell how you feel about the text, and why.

GENRE **Informational text** gives facts about a topic.